D.C. POLICE STORIES 3

DC Police Stories Three
Copyright © 2019 by Marco Kittrell
Contact Marco Kittrell: www.dcpolicestories1.net

All rights reserved. No part of this book may be reproduced in any written, electronic, recording, or photocopying without written permission of the publisher or author. The exception would be in the case of brief quotations embodied in the critical articles or reviews and pages where permission is specifically granted by the publisher or author. Contact:
J2B Publishing,
4251 Columbia Park Road,
Pomfret, MD 20675
www.J2BLLC.com
202-557-8097

Cover Design and Interior Design by Mary Barrows

Cover background image used under license from Shutterstock.com
Photo ID: 568143784 / By alexkich

Book is set in Garamond

ISBN: 978-1-948747-58-5

D.C. POLICE STORIES 3

**Lt. Marco F. Kittrell
MPDC Retired**

J2B Publishing

Also by

LT. MARCO F. KITTRELL, MPDC, (RET)

DC Police Stories

DC Police Stories Two

– The Dedication –

This book is dedicated to my fellow police officers that have served and made so many sacrifices to their respective communities. For without your continued service and courage, the world be a different place. I know the time and effort that you have committed to your careers and for the betterment of your respective police departments. I also, would like to thank the citizens of Washington, D.C. for their continued support of your efforts. For without them, we couldn't succeed in our mission. They are the reason for our being; to serve.

Lt. Marco F. Kittrell, MPDC, (RET)

6

– ACKNOWLEDGMENTS –

Once again, I must always give thanks to my wife Dorothy. She is the person that always encouraged me to write about my police career. Without her, these three books wouldn't have been written. She is my guiding light. I also, would like to remember my children and grandchildren, for they are the reason for my drive. My mom, Mrs. Betty Scott Kittrell, will always be in my heart as my founding base for success in life. Love you mom, miss you more.

Table of Contents

The Dedication 5

Acknowledgments 7

Introduction 11

CHAPTER ONE - The Alley Chase 13

CHAPTER TWO - Molly 19

CHAPTER THREE - The Female Sniper 25

CHAPTER FOUR - The President's Cousin 31

CHAPTER FIVE - The Car Shooting 35

CHAPTER SIX - I Love My Wife 39

CHAPTER SEVEN - The Search Warrant 43

CHAPTER EIGHT - The Police Officer That Froze 49

CHAPTER NINE - The Armed Robbery Gone Bad 53

CHAPTER TEN - The Station Clerk 57

CHAPTER ELEVEN - The Good Lieutenant 61

CHAPTER TWELVE - The Foot Chase 65

Chapter Thirteen - The Husband and the Wife 69

Chapter Fourteen - The Train Station Fight 73

Chapter Fifteen - The Carry-Out Shop Incident 79

Chapter Sixteen - The Two Bad Police Officers 83

Chapter Seventeen - The Good Students 87

Chapter Eighteen - The Good Nurse 91

Chapter Nineteen - The Funeral 95

Chapter Twenty - The Student 99

INTRODUCTION

This is my third book outlining some of the police cases that I was involved in. Every story is true. I just changed the names and places of the incidents, but they all occurred in Washington, D.C.

I always took every assignment very cautiously, for at any time, you or someone could be injured or even killed. No assignment is the same and if you took things as the norm, it could cause pain to many innocent people.

The rule of the day is always to go home to your family and grow old gracefully with the one you love.

Chapter One
THE ALLEY CHASE

We were working the late shift and it was approximately 8:30 PM. My partner and I were patrolling the 2700 block of Martin Luther King Avenue, Southeast., It was a very beautiful night and extremely quiet. On too many occasions, this was always a bad sign to me. On these nights, "hell was about to break open," I use to say.

My partner stated that he was hungry and wanted to eat at his favorite place. It was a very small restaurant and if you saw it, you probably wouldn't stop there to eat, but their food was the best in the city and always full of people. Everyone in that part of town ate there and the prices were reasonable. You always had to stand in line in order to get a seat and eat your meal, but, no one ever complained about the wait. The food was that good.

I used to laugh when the waitresses and cooks would argue over the food, the wait, and how much time it took to get drinks. Everyone in the restaurant would get into the act, including the customers. They would be so funny; I wish I could have videotaped the conversations between them.

People would say things like,

"How long is it going to take to get a meal in this place, before next year?"

The waitresses always replied,

"You can get the hell out and go home, if you have one."

People never left, they just waited. The food was that good and the right price, cheap.

We finally got a table and as always, it happened. The police dispatcher stated that an arm robbery was in progress and shots had been fired. To make things worse, the incident was only three blocks from our location. I thought I had heard a noise that sounded like gun shots, but with all the noise in the restaurant, I couldn't hear it clearly. With so much vehicle traffic on the street, this also made the sound very faint. I should have exited the restaurant and investigated further when I first heard the sound. This was a mistake that I wouldn't make again as a police officer. I admit that by this time, with two years under my belt as a police officer, while I might be hungry, I never neglected my duties. I had thrown many meals away in response to police calls. This was just another one of those days.

My partner looked at his meal and said,

"Got dam, again. Can we just get a break?", and he then said, "let's go Kittrell".

We inform the dispatcher that we were in the area and responding to the alarm. As we were exiting the restaurant, one of the waitresses said,

"Two seats are open, and the food is already on the table and hot."

Several people attempted to get our seats. I told my partner as we are running towards our police car,

"That is a dam shame, no respect, they could have saved our food until we returned."

The Alley Chase

As we drove off, the persons that were eating our food said very loudly, "Thanks, Officers. Go get them!"

Everyone in the restaurant started laughing. My partner and I even laughed.

As we are driving towards the assignment with the sirens and lights blasting, my partner said,

"Kittrell, do you know how long it is going to take us to get another seat in that place and get a meal? A very long time and I am hungry as hell. I should have taken some of those dam hard rolls."

We just laughed; we both were hungry.

We arrived on the scene quickly as we were so close. Another police unit arrived as we entered the liquor store with our guns out. We observed a man, who I will name Mr. John Smith, on the floor. It appeared that he had been shot in the arm, the wound was not that grave, and he was talking.

His wife, who was standing over him, was attempting to render comfort and aid. We informed the dispatcher and requested an ambulance for Mr. Smith and a detective unit to assist.

Ms. Smith stated that two men had entered their store, produced handguns, and demanded money. Her husband was attempting to open the register when for no reason one of the suspects shot him in the arm. The man opened the register, stole approximately $400, and they then fled on foot.

We further informed the dispatcher of the circumstances and broadcast a look-out for the suspects. We began searching for them because other units had arrived and were processing the crime scene.

My partner suggested that we canvas a certain area that drug users frequent. We might get lucky, in that the area was very near to the scene of the robbery. On the way, we happen to drive by the restaurant that we had departed hastily and where we had left our meal. As we drive by, the two gentlemen that had gotten our seats, were still eating and they were now eating our chocolate cakes. They even waved at us as we drove by.

I said, "That is a dam shame. No respect. I am so hungry."

My partner also said, "So am I."

We finally arrived where the area was saturated with drug users. I questioned one of the prostitutes that I knew. I will call her Molly. I had use her on many occasions for information. She has been walking the streets for one year. I arrested a guy who assaulted her with a gun a year ago. She always remembered me and helped with providing information with guys who carried weapons. We made many arrests.

She said she had just arrived in the last 15 minutes. She said, "Look under the light on the corner behind you," and then walk away very slowly. As Molly walked away, she said, "Fuck off! You police are no good." This was to mask our conversation.

There were eight people on the corner and one of them matched the description of the suspect that had shot Mr. Smith. We called for backup and waited another few minutes, not to make the suspect too suspicious.

A few minutes go by and once the other units were in position, my partner and I exited our police vehicle. It was at that time, that the suspect started running towards the alley and the chase was on. My partner and I were both young men and could catch most people.

As we give chase, all the other people in the area, stood back. One of the persons said,

The Alley Chase

"Look at those mothers run; they should be ball players."

In the alley, we notice that there were no lights. Drug dealers had broken all the lights in the area, so they couldn't be seen selling drugs. We lost sight of the suspect. Realizing that he could be armed, we proceeded with caution, with our guns out.

The other police units were entering the opposite side of the alley. We had informed the dispatcher of our location prior to entering the alley. Knowing that other police officers were entering the alley, we stayed at our present location, just in case the suspect attempted to exit at our location. We didn't want to get involved in a shooting while police were on opposite side. We knew of prior incidents where this had occurred.

Suddenly, the suspect emerged from behind a trash container, jumped on the both of us, and knocked my partner to the ground. I lost my balance, but didn't fall. I could see that the suspect wasn't arm, so I holstered my weapon and the fight was on. I must say the suspect was very strong and giving us all the fight, we could handle. I call for assistance to the other officers in the alley. They started running towards us. It seemed like they were 100 miles away. Any police officer who has been in that situation can relate.

Then suddenly the suspect attempts to pull a gun from his pocket. I lost my balance and fell and was attempting to un-holster my firearm, in order to protect myself and partner. My partner then struck the suspect with his radio to the face knocking him to the ground and the gun fell out of his hand to the ground. By this time, I had recovered and then handcuffed the suspect.

He was transported back to the scene and was identified by Mrs. Smith and the other witnesses as the shooter. Later investigation revealed the second suspect. The gun was matched to the bullet that was removed from Mr. Smith.

Three days later my partner and I went back to that restaurant and to our surprise we were greeted with an open table. The waitress who had served us on the earlier day knew we were coming and saved us a table.

She said, "Officers, don't get used to this good treatment," and laughed and said, "Thanks for catching those mothers. Also, your meal was paid for by the two guys who ate your last meal. They didn't buy the cake; they had a limit."

I saw Molly a few days later and she said she was going back home to Alabama. She was tired of her life. I wished her well and I never spoke with her again. I hope she made it. She wasn't a bad person, just chose the wrong profession.

I really enjoyed my job during the early years. I miss working with those guys in the section.

Chapter Two
MOLLY

Let's talk about Molly. She was a very young girl, only 22 years old, and from Alabama. I first met Molly in 1975. She had been assaulted by a man with a handgun. He hit Molly on her left leg. They were arguing over money. Molly was a prostitute.

My partner and I were driving in the 2500 Block of Talbert Street, Southeast, and I observed the assault. We stopped the vehicle, jumped out, and subdued the suspect without incident. The suspect didn't see us coming. Molly observed us arriving and kept the suspect occupied by holding onto him. We were also aware of the fact that the suspect had a gun in his hand, but Molly did a very good job of keeping his attention.

The suspect was subdued, and Molly began telling her story. Molly reported that she and the suspect were quarreling over money. Suddenly, the suspect produced a gun and struck Molly to the leg. He wanted to pay less than Molly requested for her services.

The suspect and Molly were arrested and then treated for their injuries. During the trial the suspect was given six months and Molly was release for lack of evidence. The suspect didn't want to testify against Molly.

As Molly is walking out the court room, she tells me that she appreciated my partner and I for helping her. From then on, whenever she knows of a person carrying a weapon, she would tell us. She wanted those no-good men off the street. This began her relationship as a police informant.

Every week thereafter, I would go to the location where Molly worked and inquire if anyone was carrying a firearm. We had a code. She would walk by someone and look in the other direction and scratch her noise. We would wait a few minutes and walk towards the subject. Always, the subject with the gun would run and we always caught the subject and recovered a weapon. We made several arrest in this manner. In some cases, the subject would throw their gun to the ground as they ran. We recovered three firearms in this fashion.

On one occasion, after receiving the signal from Molly, I recognized the person in question. He was a dangerous person with a long criminal background. He was also suspected of several shootings involving drug gangs. We approached this case much differently. The suspect, Mike, was a known shooter and I didn't think he would run away. We could have a shooting on our hands and I wanted to go home to my family. We needed back-up and plenty of it as this guy was dangerous.

We informed the dispatcher and requested back-up. A plan was established and we had all the exits covered. But Mike, was a professional criminal and I could tell that he was getting very suspicious. Those from the criminal elements think and sleep crime and are always suspicious of everyone.

Prior to exiting our vehicle, we notice that Mike was walking away and towards large crowds. We informed the other units that were in the area. Two undercover officers inform us that they will go into the crow and attempt to confront Mike without incident.

As the undercover officers made their way into the crowd. Mike starts walking faster, as to say that he knows the police are about to close in on him. One of the undercover offices forgot to turn his radio volume down and Mike heard the transmission.

Mike pulled his firearm from his pants pocket and starts running through the crowd. The crowd panicked and everyone starts running in every direction. All the police officers in the area join in the chase. I just knew that Mike was going to start shooting and some innocent person would get shot and possibly killed. I had seen this too many times.

Mike slipped on the wet surface and, as he was falling, he started shooting at the police officers. The gun fight was on. Several officers involved in the foot chase returned fire. Bullets were going everywhere. Fortunately, there were no civilians in the alley.

My partner and I took cover behind some parked vehicles on the street. There were too many police officers shooting in the alley and we couldn't get into the fight because of the bullets that were coming in our direction by the other police officers. I counted five officers firing. I said to myself, I now knew what military people go through when they are involved in combat.

I could see Mike laying on the ground firing at the officers and no shots were taking effect on Mike or the officers. Then suddenly, the gun battle stopped. Mike threw his weapon down on the ground and stated, "Officers, stop firing, please. I give up. Please, I don't want to die."

The officers stopped firing and gave Mike directions to lay on the ground with his hands in plain view. Mike complied with the directions and kept saying, "Please don't shoot me, please."

The officers approached Mike with their firearms pointing at him. He was handcuffed without incident. No one was injured. I told my partner

I thought over 50 shots were fired and luckily no one was hit. It was Mike's and the officer's lucky day.

As we were processing the crime scene, Molly walked by and gave me a signal that she wanted to speak with me later. We had a system, previously established, for when she had information to give me.

I met Molly two hours later at our normal spot. It was several blocks from her working area.

She said, "Kittrell, that was a hell of a fight. I didn't see you or your partner shoot anybody. You were too busy hiding behind those cars. I don't blame you; bullets were everywhere. I'm just glad you are okay."

I just smiled and thanked her for the information.

She further stated, "That mother fucker was always beating up the girls and threating them. When he was confronted with real men, he cried like a little bitch. They should have killed that little pig."

We talk further and I told her to stay out of trouble. As she was walking away, I said, "Molly, why are you walking these streets? You are a smart girl. You can do better." She looked at me and smiled, saying she only had a little more time and then she was going back home to Alabama. I just looked at her as she walked away

I kept an eye on her and all the girls. They never caused any problems. I knew what they were doing was illegal and, on many occasions, they would be arrested, even Molly, during police undercover operations. I always provided the judge in question with Molly's undercover work. This was allowed by the department.

Molly continued helping me with my gun cases and a year later she moved back to Alabama. Mike was found guilty of several crimes and served several years in jail. The gun that he had use in the shooting was connected to other crimes that he had committed earlier.

Mike died in 1992; murdered by a rival gang member. He was shot 12 times. It was later learned during the investigation that it was a retaliation killing for all the bad things that he had committed earlier in his life. That is another story.

Chapter Three
THE FEMALE SNIPER

Officer Gloria Mason was 25 years old and joined the police department four years ago. She was very bright, motivated, and wanted to succeed in the department. Her goal was to be part of the department's Emergency Response Unit. They handle all the barricades and serious incidents where several different types of weapons might be needed. She wanted to be part of the real action, as she saw it.

She worked in the patrol section and made many arrests for only being in the department for four years. She was exposed to many different types of serious incidents. As an officer in the city, it was very difficult not to be.

She used to say, "I wanted to be the person that saves the day; the person that rides into town and makes everything ok."

The older officer always said, "Be careful what you ask for, you might get it."

She was a little aggressive, but a good officer.

Then it happened. She applied for the Emergency Response Unit and she was selected for the position. She was so excited and couldn't wait to go through the training process. When she was given her new uniforms, she came back to her old section and proudly presented them to the other officers. Everyone was happy for her. They all joked with Gloria, telling her, "Everyone better watch out, Gloria is going to be a sharpshooter."

But Gloria took her new position seriously and wanted to be the best in her field.

During her training, Gloria perform exceptionally scoring higher than any of the male officers in all the required categories. Even the commander of the unit commented on Gloria's success. Her scores were at the very top. During these times, women still had to prove themselves every day. It had been less than eleven years since the department started assigning women to the patrol sections, as we used to say, "working on the streets." Yes, there were very prejudiced people in the department during those days. They were on both sides of the fence, but they were all proven wrong about many things. That is another story to tell.

I attended Gloria's graduation ceremony. She looked like she had just won the lottery. Everyone was very proud of her success. Her entire family was there. Love and kisses were plenty and well received by all present.

She told me, "Sgt. Kittrell, a new sheriff is in town."

I just smiled and wished her well. I wanted Gloria to be reach her goal. She further told me that she was going to make all the officers in the old section proud of her by doing well.

Once assigned to an Emergency Response Unit squad, she was in her own world. She was the first officer through the door and the last one to leave.

When we spoke about her encounters, I told her, "Just do your job, don't be no hero, and don't take unnecessary chances in life. You have already proven yourself."

The Female Sniper

She told me, "Sergeant, they are always looking at me, trying to screw me up. I know that I'm in a man's outfit."

For the next two years, Gloria performed her job without incident. I still thought she was trying too hard, but I did understand her feeling about her position.

The following year she was reassigned to the sniper's unit. Now, you had to be very good to get that position. Your scores had to be twice as good as the other regular officers to qualify and Gloria was that good when it came to firearms. Many women, at first, had problems qualifying in that many of them never fired a weapon before. But, once they received training, the majority of them passed, just like men, who were in the same category.

As in many cases, an officer has an experience on the job that changes their perspective about the job. I had many, another story. Gloria reported to duty Monday morning. They were scheduled to be at the range all day, but like in many cases on the job, things change, and this day would be one that changed Gloria completely. As the squad was about to exit the station and report to the range, the call came in. They were needed. Two people had been shot and a third person was being held hostage in their home.

The squad immediately responded and on their arrival at the crime scene they went into action as their training dictated. As they were preparing to enter the home and secure the hostage, the negotiator was attempting to calm the suspect down and have him release his hostage. During the briefing, it was learned that the suspect had entered the home and shot two men, who were brothers. It was later learned that the suspect wanted the hostage, his girlfriend, to leave the home with him. After she refused, he shot the two men and threaten to kill his girlfriend.

Gloria was assigned as a sniper and had a clear shot at the suspect. He was holding a gun in his hand as he was talking to the negotiator. The hostage was laying on the floor crying. It also appeared that she had been shot in the leg.

Gloria reports what she has observed to the field commander and stands by for further instructions. As the supervisors are debating their next move, Gloria reports that the suspect is standing over the hostage pointing his gun; indication that he is going to shoot her.

Furthermore, the suspect is telling the negotiator that his life is over and there is no going back, as he is standing over the hostage.

This information is immediately transmitted to the commander on the scene. Fearing for the safety of the hostage, he orders that the suspect be shot at the earliest opportunity. Gloria acknowledges her directions and seconds later she fires her weapon, striking the suspect to the head, killing him instantly. Gloria reports her actions and the entry team forces the front and secures the hostages. All three injured person are transported to the hospital, are treated, and release.

Gloria goes through the department's process when an officer is involved in a police shooting, including being examined by the police doctors. She is exonerated. I called Gloria later, checking on her well-being, and told her about my two police shootings and how they affected me.

I could tell that Gloria wasn't ok. She didn't sound like the person that I knew. Many people think taking someone's life is easy, especially when you are doing your job. But it is a burden to most people and I think Gloria was having issues with the incident. She took some time off from the job to get herself together.

She reported back to work a few months later and she sounded like her old self. We had lunch one day, but I could tell that she still wasn't there completely.

She said, "Sergeant Kittrell, I can still see that guy's face in my scope. Killing isn't easy, even when you are saving a life. I see that face every night."

We talked about another hour and we departed.

Gloria stayed in her present assignment for another four years. She was promoted to sergeant three years later and retired in 2005. She married while in the department to a fireman, had three children, and is now a grandparent, doing well in life. Great job to an outstanding person!

Chapter Four
THE PRESIDENT'S COUSIN

Every now and then you, as a police officer, will have an incident that will surprise you. I have had the privilege during my career to meet numerous people of all backgrounds. On many occasions, I was stunned by meeting them; Presidents, movie stars, sport figures, and other very important people. But this day I will always remember as the one that guides me today.

In other words, no matter how a person looks you can never judge them by their appearance. I was working the day shift and having a very busy day. As my partner and I were making our way back to the police station to turn in some paperwork, we were reassigned to a theft complaint. My partner stated that it appears we are the only one's working today. We acknowledged the dispatcher and responded to the address. On our arrival, we are approached by the store owner. He was furious. He reported that a homeless man entered his store, stole a package of ham, and was outside eating the stolen item in front of the store.

My partner and I offered to pay for the item and the store owner refused. He further stated that he is exhausted of the same person stealing from his store weekly and he wanted to press charges. We continued to discuss options other than arresting the person, but the store owner refused. He was just disgusted with all the thefts from his store by all the homeless people in the area.

Therefore, we had no choice and we arrested the homeless man and I will call him John. As we are talking to John, I noticed that he had a very good vocabulary. I wasn't too surprised, because many of the homeless men were educated people. Most of them had some dynamic incident in their life that caused them to live on the streets. I knew one of Kennedy's sons was one of these persons. I used to see him walking the streets and I would think, all that money and you would never know it. There were many cases; attorneys, military people with distinguished careers, business people, and all types of professions. People who had great careers and now they were living on the streets.

In some cases, I would talk to these people and they would amaze me with their education and background. Now, there were others on the opposite side of that coin. People who had very said lives and wanted to live on the streets; too many to count. Several of these people used illegal drugs, had mental issues, and were dangerous people, but majority of them were harmless.

We transported John back to the police station for processing. As we are about to begin processing procedures, John stated that he was a lawyer and he wanted to make a phone call. He further stated that he wanted to call the President of the United States. Several of the officers in the station started laughing. I even smiled; we have heard this before.

I told John he could make the phone call after we completed the paperwork. John said, ok, and he apologized for the incident. If he knew that the store owner was going to have him arrested, he said he would have walked back to the homeless shelter. He felt that the owner didn't mind him eating the ham, in that he had been doing so for several weeks without incident.

We allow John to make his phone call and I noticed that the number was to the Secret Service Agency. John tells them that he has been arrested and briefed them on the situation and then hangs up the phone. A few minutes later, we get a phone call from the Chief of Police Office and we are directed to assist the secret service on their arrival. We are all in shock.

John looked at me and said, "I mean to be no problem to you or your agency. I was just hungry. The President is my First Cousin."

He also told me that he had a nervous breakdown when his mother and father died in an airplane crash. Shortly before that, his wife and daughter were killed by a drunk driver. He just couldn't live with all that tragedy in his life. The President and he were raised together and he took care of him when he got in trouble.

The Secret Service agents arrived at the police station and they are briefed by my partner and me. The agents inform us that John is the President's cousin and ask if they could speak with the store owner. My supervisor approves the requests and shortly after their meeting, the owner agreed to be reimbursed and not press charges against John.

John apologized to all the police officers and he stated that he wouldn't steal again. The agents and John leave the station and John never stole anything else that I was aware of.

I learned many years later that John died and the President in question was out of office and he paid for and attended the funeral. May John finally rest in peace.

Chapter Five
THE CAR SHOOTING

Officer Tony Johnson was working the day shift and it was approximately 9:30 AM. He was having a very good day. Nothing unusual for a day shift other than the normal problems. Officer Johnson had been a Police Officer for five years and doing very well. He was cramming for the sergeant's examination which was schedule to be taken in six months. He was also very excited in that he and his wife were expecting their first child in two months. Everything was going well for the officer and his life.

The officer received an assignment for a burglary report. As he is driving towards the address, he observed a vehicle driving at a high rate of speed in the opposite direction. The officer attempts to stop the vehicle by sounding his siren and flashing his red lights. The vehicle in question starts driving even faster.

The officer informs the dispatcher and other police units join in the chase. By this time the vehicle in question is driving at a very high rate of speed and in a reckless manner. The vehicle is being operated and occupied by two subjects. During the chase, subject number two, who is in the passenger's seat, points a gun at the officers and starts firing at them. Several shots strike their vehicles, but none of the officers are struck. The officers don't return fire. Training dictates that they aren't allowed to fire at moving vehicles, unless someone's life is in danger.

As the officers' attempt to catch the speeding vehicle, a roadblock is established in order to stop the vehicle. The vehicle in question suddenly makes a U-turn and starts driving towards the pursuing police vehicles. Realizing the danger, the police vehicles maneuver in order not to strike the approaching speeding vehicle.

Amazingly, the speeding vehicle avoided hitting the police vehicles and makes another turn down the adjacent street. The police vehicle give chase. The suspect starts firing his gun again at the officers.

One of the police vehicles gets so close that they can maneuver the speeding vehicle into a one-way street. Now, the normal traffic is approaching the speeding vehicle as the police vehicles are close behind.

Suddenly, the approaching traffic stops and the speeding vehicle is blocked in. The police vehicles enclose the area. Now we have a situation. We have trapped two arm suspects, who have already proven to be very dangerous, in a vehicle.

A supervisor arrives on the scene and directs the officers to hold their fire. You now have several civilians behind the suspects and if gun fire erupts, they could possibly be injured. But, the suspects for some unknown reason remain calm.

The sergeant exits his vehicle and directs the suspects to turn their vehicle off, toss the car keys on the ground, and surrender. By this time the majority of the other officers have also exited their vehicles and surrounded the suspects with their weapons pointing at the vehicle in question. Other officers were attempting to redirect the civilians behind the scene to a safe location.

The Car Shooting

A few seconds go by and once the civilians are out of danger the sergeant repeats his directions to the suspects. The suspects are still in the vehicle and looking around, as to be analyzing the situation. The longer it took, the worse the situation was about to become.

Suddenly, the suspects attempt to break through the police barriers and police vehicles. They drive towards them and both suspects start firing again. Now all hell breaks out and all the police officers started firing at the vehicle, fearing for their lives. The suspects then drive into a brick wall, knocking themselves semiconscious. The officers rush in and subdue the suspects. No shots took effect.

The suspects were arrested, treated for their injuries, and processed. We later learned that the suspect had just committed an arm robbery and shot the clerk in the store. Officer Johnson observed the suspects as they were making good their escape. The suspect's firearms were later identified as weapons used in other robberies throughout the Washington Area.

After all the shots that were fired and all the vehicles driving at a high rate of speed, no injuries other than the suspects and no serious damage to property. Normally, it is the opposite. Thank God no innocent people were injured. The store owner recovered from his wounds.

Officer Johnson was given a commendation for his action. The officer was later promoted to sergeant after scoring high on the sergeant's examination. He and his wife had a beautiful, healthy baby girl. The sergeant retired in 1999 and relocated to North Carolina.

DC Police Stories 3

Chapter Six
I LOVE MY WIFE

As a police officer, you run across many different situations and people. During my career, I have met my share. My partner John Smith was one of those people. He had been a police officer for five years and doing very well. John was married to a very beautiful women and had two children. Everything appeared to be good, but appearances can be misleading. In the police world, it can be common place.

One day, John and I were having lunch. John had been quiet all day and this was out of place for him. It was a very busy day and John always made jokes about some of the cases that we were involved in. He was not making fun of the people, just helping to make the day go by.

I finally ask John if he was okay. John looked at me and said that his marriage was going to hell. His wife was cheating. I didn't know what to say. I have seen this before with many other police officers but didn't expect it with John. Police officers don't have a good record when it comes to marriage. John was now in that long line with others who had bad family relationships. I had just gotten a divorce, so I could relate.

Many police officers are their own worst enemies. Between women, liquor, the pressures of the job, it wasn't easy living a normal life. I used to see officers do the things that were just terrible, when it came to be a married man. But that is another story. In every case, the officers were getting divorces.

Now John was different. He loved his wife, went home every night, never cheated on his wife and he had his entire life planned. He was going to work for 25 years, retire with his wife, and love those grandkids. John loved his children and would do anything to enhance their future. He wanted two more kids, but his wife wanted to put time in her career.

John further tells me, "Kittrell my life has gone to shit. I thought I had it all, but life plays games with you."

I just said I was sorry. I didn't want to push the matter. Policemen and women have a very soft spot with most policemen. I could tell that John was in pain. He wanted his family back and I couldn't give it to him.

I tell John that maybe if you and your wife just sit down and have a talk maybe everything will be okay.

John said, "Hell no. She has been sleeping with other men. Not just one, but others."

Now, I don't know what to say after that comment. I'm getting concern because John has a look on his face that I have seen too many times on other police officers' faces. It's a crazy look and people have gotten hurt, even killed.

I ask John what his plans were. I'm attempting to think of something to tell my friend, because of my concern for him and his family. Before I could say anything else, John hits the table with his hands so hard everyone in the restaurant stopped talking and looked at us. Now, I'm really scared for john.

I love My Wife

That look on his face has gone from sadness to rage. John starts crying. I pay the check and we leave the restaurant. None of the patrons say anything and I just let John get it out. I'm thinking what my next move will be, but all of a sudden John stopped crying, looks at me and said," Fuck it, I'm leaving tonight".

We talk further and I'm just trying to figure John out where his mind is. I have seen too many police officers do crazy things when confronted with such issues.

John was no different and I wasn't going to l let John go without me being satisfied that he was ok. I wasn't about to let my friend go down without a fight. I just have seen too many bad things happen in my police career.

We check off and I offered to take John home. He refused. We talk further. I really wanted to take him home, just to feel him out further. I have seen too many officers go down that bad road and never return to reality. Bad things happen. Police shootings, assaults, children hurt, and even people killed.

John said that everything was okay and don't worry about him. He would never hurt his wife and especially never his children. Even with all the hurt, he still loved that dam women. John drives off and I said a prayer for the family and myself.

I called John at home several hours later and his wife, Joan, answered the phone. I just made some small talk and ask if I could speak with John. Joan tells me that he was sleeping, but he would call when he awakens. I said thanks and was glad that they weren't fighting. John calls me later that night and thanks me. He said everything was okay and he was planning to take a few days off to take care of his family.

John took two weeks off and I didn't hear or see him until he returned to duty. He looked good and sounded like his old self. I wanted to ask about his wife, but I didn't think it was my place. If he was happy, we all must live with ourselves. It wasn't for me to judge another man.

We worked the entire tour and didn't speak about his wife. As we check off of duty and walk out the police station, John stopped, looks at me, and said, "I forgave my wife. I want my family."

I said, "Great. I wish you and your family the very best."

We never spoke of the incident again for the next 20 years. John retired in 1996. He and his wife are still happily married, have six grandchildren, and live in the Washington, DC, Area.

Chapter Seven
THE SEARCH WARRANT

Now I have a story for you. I was the commander of a Vice Enforcement Unit. The investigators were good. They were self-motivated, reliable, and loyal to the mission. The supervisors were even better. They stayed on top of their investigators and their cases. They never let me down and always kept me informed of their cases.

I had my checks and balances, but rarely had to use them as a commander. The unit was always on target. I had a good unit and, even better, a great job that I loved. I felt that we were making a difference in the community. People were selling poison to our kids and in some cases, there were deaths.

I used to get so angry at parents who were addicted to drugs and their children suffered badly. I have seen children go without food and other basic needs that most people would take unsurprisingly, as nature behavior. I have seen people leave their children at home for days, without supervision, which lead to other problems in the households.

One of the worst cases was when a parent sold his daughter for drugs. That was the one time when I could have lost my job. The child was only 13 years old and she was abused by another drug user. Luckily, the case was closed with several arrests very early in the commission of the crime.

Thank God someone did the proper thing and reported the activity to the police. We jumped on the case immediately and brought the matter to a closure. The child in question was saved even thou she had to be treated for several other issues.

Some of the drug dealers even used children to facilitate their drug activities. I mean every aspect of the drug trade; selling, transportation, using, lookouts, and runners. There were no avenues that they wouldn't utilize. On several occasions, the children were so young that they didn't know what they were doing. These cases always caught our attention in the early stages of the criminal activities. We would also jump on these cases very quickly and bring these activities to a closure with arrests, and seizures of guns, money and illegal drugs.

One case was brought to our attention that drugs were being sold out of a house. I assigned the case to Sergeant Mike Williams and his squad. They were very good in addressing these types of crimes. They could get evidence on any premises that were selling drugs. There are certain items that are needed in order to ascertain an arrest and search warrant and the sergeant and his people always met those requirements. They were very good.

During the investigation, evidence was established very quickly and search warrants were obtained. Prior to the execution of the warrants, the investigators prepare a plan for the execution. Everyone is given an assignment, safety first, and other measures are taken to ensure that no one is injured. A supervisor is always part of the briefing, approves the same, and is present during the execution of the warrant. The unit had been very successful in implementing such measures; therefore, I expected the same results.

The Search Warrant

On the day of the execution of the warrant, everything was in place. The officers were even joking that this would be another successful operation. Not to the detriment of the mission, just trying to relax everyone, it was a police ritual, but everyone was still focus to the mission.

It wasn't good to get too relaxed. People have been hurt or even killed when that happened; too many cases to count. Taking the attitude "same as usual" will cause someone to get hurt.

At the end of the joking session, the sergeant always said, "Alright, let's get focused and get this thing done. Everyone put their game face on."

One of the investigators stated, smiling, "Sergeant loves that speech. He should get it patented."

The officers approached the house in question. They set up for execution and the sergeant gives the order to kick the door in. As they are attempting to force the door, it fails to open. We knew the investigation had revealed the type of security the drug dealers were using. We felt that we had adequate equipment to force the door. But the door wouldn't open after several more attempts to force the same.

You could hear the occupants inside the premise moving around, making noise, and statements, "They are coming, quick, move everything." Now safety is the number one issue. We had learned that the drug dealers had weapons inside and we were prepared for anything. The officers were well armed to address the threat.

The sergeant now directs the officer to use a tool (I am not allowed to identify it because of the nature of the tool) that is still utilized today in police operation. The door is finally forced opened and the officers make their entry without incident.

Amazingly, all the occupants surrender without firing a shot. This was a relief. The house and occupants are secured as per police protocols. During the search, no weapons or illegal drugs are located. The information that was gathered and verified by other sources indicated that those items were present.

At the time of the execution of the warrant, there was a senior citizen in a wheelchair. She was identified as one of the suspects' grandmother. The officers had searched the wheelchair and the grandmother and nothing was found. The officer that conducted the search was a young female and she admitted that she didn't perform a complete search, as indicated in her training. The officer in question was detailed to the unit to get acquainted with drug operations within the police departments. This was a normal process at the time.

The sergeant directs that another search of the grandmother be performed. As they are about to conduct the search, the grandson asks that he be allowed to speak with his grandparent. He tells her to give the officers all the weapons and drugs. She complies and turns over two firearms and several bags containing illegal drugs. They were all hidden within her clothes. The officers still conducted a further search and recovered $5,000 in cash.

The lesson that all present learned was it is just good business to never assume anything and always monitor the actions of others. The suspects were arrested and gave further evidence on other operations, in order that the grandmother wouldn't be charge for her part in the crime.

Later investigation revealed that during drug transactions the suspects would hide the grandmother in another location in the house and her presence was never identified. After this incident, the unit put in place action plans to rectify any further mistakes concerning these types of issues.

Chapter Eight
The Police Officer That Froze

Officer Tom Scott was a good police officer and performing very well. He had been an officer for six years. He came from a police family; his father and grandfather had both retired from the Metropolitan Police Department. Tom was a single man and love being so.

Tom always spoke of his family and some of their adventures as policemen. He really respected their accomplishments. I always encourage him to write a book about his family as I enjoyed the stories. Both of his fathers were investigators and investigated many serious crimes, not only in the city but other locations as well.

Speaking with Tom sometimes gave me the belief that he was living in their shadows. Many policemen throughout the area knew Tom's family and their history. People would always say,

"Tom, you should be proud of your family, they were good policemen."

I don't believe Tom always received the comments well. He would just smile and say thank you.

Tom and I were having lunch one day at our favorite location. He told me that it was difficult living in the shadow of his fathers as people would compare him to them. On certain occasions, officers would say things that could be even insulting. It made Tom feel that he wasn't equal to his fathers' accomplishments. I don't believe the officers were attempting to be abusive, it just made Tom uncomfortable.

On several assignments, I felt Tom was taking too many chances in that he was not performing his duties as he had been trained. Most police officers are injured, or even killed because, they fail to perform their duties as indicated by their training.

I noticed that on several assignments and even when firearms were involved, Tom wouldn't wait for his back-up police officers before responding to the incidents. I mentioned my concerns to Tom, but he just said, don't worried about it, they were all milk runs, (easy assignments). I told Tom that we had been policemen long enough to know that any assignment could be your last. We should take them all seriously or it might just be your last. Tom and I continued talking about the issue, but he just said, "Don't worried about. I know what I am doing."

Most police officers we have a little cockiness in them, including myself. You can get so confident in your abilities that you forget about reality. On many occasions, I had to take a step back and look at myself and my surroundings. In doctors, they call it the "I'm God" syndrome. Too many victories aren't good. This is just my opinion, some might disagree. I always liked a little setback sometimes, in police work, as it keeps you focused on the mission and not yourself. But this rational is another story to tell at another time.

On this day we were confronted with a situation that Tom and I never forgot. We received an assignment for a very large group fight. They had some type of weapons, mostly sticks and bats. On our arrival, we observed several people fighting in the middle of the street. By this time,

The Police Officer That Froze

other police units had arrived and we all attempted to subdue the situation. There were only six people fighting and we had adequate personal on the scene to address the situation.

As we are making arrests and attempting to process the suspects, a very large crowd, approximately 80 people, suddenly approached us and started throwing rocks and bottles at the officers. Now we have a serious problem. We have ten police officers, six of them occupied with arrests, confronted with a very large mob. We call for assistance and attempt to leave the area. In most cases involving large crowds, it is best to leave the area and address the situation when you have adequate personnel to address the problem. During this era, the area in question, was having problems with the police and was known for minor riots. They would erupt abruptly, for any incident involving the police.

As we are about to leave the area, I noticed that Tom was still seating in his police vehicle. I realize that he never exited the vehicle during the conflict. I motioned to him to leave the area immediately and he acted as if he didn't see me. I know that he observed my signal, because he was looking directly in my eyes. Another officer knocked on Tom's window and told him to get the hell out of the area. Tom acknowledge the officer and drove off. We were able to maintain control of the prisoners and they were transported to the police station for processing.

In incidents of this nature, the police assign Community Police Officers, who are trained to handle such incidents, to resolve the issues in the community that caused the minor riot. In most cases the issues are addressed and the community goes back to being normal. During those times, unrest in certain communities were a serious problem. Training for the officers addressed many issues and the attitude for the police department had to change also and it worked. In today's police departments, Community Policing it is tradition now; great thing.

After the prisoners were processed and things in the community calmed down, Tom and I checked off for duty. We went to my house to have a drink. I asked Tom what happen. As he is holding his glass, he looks at me and said,

"Kittrell, I don't know what happen. After all the shit we have seen, it hit me when I saw all those people throwing rocks and bottles at us. I'm really sorry to let the guys down."

I told him, to just let it go, we all have our moments on the job. We continued to talk for another eight hours and Tom went home.

We never spoke of the incident in the next twenty years. Tom never had another episode during his career. He was awarded several commendations during his tenure as a policeman. Tom retired as a Sergeant in 2000 and his fathers were there to see their son receive his recognition. Tom finally got married, after retiring, to a wonderful woman.

In any career a person can have a bad day no manner who they are. I have had my moments, but never failed to do my job. As policemen, your life is always on the line, on or off duty. Military personnel when in combat, experience this even more than we could relate.

I never held that incident against Tom, because I knew the man, he was a good policeman. Sometimes the pressure just builds up and you have a meltdown. The character of a person is judged when they are confronted with the incident and the aftermath.

Enjoy your retirement Tom, you deserve it, you don't need to prove yourself to anyone.

Chapter Nine
THE ARMED ROBBERY GONE BAD

Mr. Ron Smith was a good man. He had been the owner of his corner store for thirty years. Everyone in the are respected and liked Ron. He was always doing good things for the people in the area, even giving them food on credit when they didn't have any money to pay for the items.

During his tenure in the area he had never been the victim of a robbery. That was about to change. It was Friday night and Ron was about to close the shop. Normally, he had another person working with him, but on this night, he was alone.

There was one customer, a male, in the shop and he was about to pay for his items. Then another male entered the store and both customers made eye contact. Ron observed their actions and this made him feel unease.

The first suspect was stalling as he was looking through his pockets for money. Then suddenly, the second suspect produced a handgun and pointed the weapon at Ron. The first suspect ran to the front door and locked the same and displayed the "We Are Closed" sign on the door.

The actions of the suspects made Ron very nervous. He thought they would just demand money and exit the store. But, in this case they wanted more. The suspects told Ron to obey their commands and everything would be okay and he wouldn't get hurt.

They take Ron to the back of the store and begin their questioning. They tell Ron that they are aware that he has a safe in the store. Ron says he does not have a safe and all he has is what is kept in the cash register.

Suspect One strikes Ron to the face with the pistol, saying, "Mother Fucker."

Suspect Two says, "We don't have all night. Give us the money, or else."

Ron starts crying and said that he wasn't going to die for money, living is to important. The suspects continued to strike Ron and threatening to kill him, if he doesn't produce the safe. Then suddenly, there was a knock at the front door. The suspects had a quick conversation and agreed that they would answer the same and lose the person. Before leaving, Suspect One tells Ron, "Don't make a sound I'll shoot you."

The suspect answerers the door and tells the person that the store is close. The person acknowledges the suspect and walks away. What the suspect didn't know is that he was speaking to an undercover officer. During the robbery, a witness observed the crime and notified the police.

The police responded, observed the suspects inside, and implemented a plan to subdue them without injuries to Ron. The undercover officer was sent in to analyze the situation. He reports back to his supervisors and they are briefed on the situation.

It is decided to enter the store before Ron could be harmed. The suspects continued their torture of Ron. Suspect One points the gun at Ron and is about to shoot him when four police officers enter the back room where Ron is being held. They surprised the suspects and the suspects surrendered without firing a shot. I guess they wanted to live. Or, maybe it was the shotguns pointing in their direction persuaded them.

The Armed Robbery Gone Bad

The suspects were arrested and Ron was transported to the hospital for treatment. It was later learned that the firearms used by the suspects were not operational. Also, Ron did have a safe in his store, but there was no money in the safe. He had deposited the money in the bank earlier that day.

The next day Ron reported back to work as if nothing had happened. Several people stopped by and wished Ron well. They even offered to be security for his shop. He declined the offer and said he wasn't going anywhere; he was here to stay.

When I retired in 1995, Ron was still there. He retired in 2000 and his son took over the business and it is still there serving the community. His son added a small restaurant. I hear the food is good. They are located on Talbert Street Southeast.

The suspects were found guilty and served several years in prison for the crimes committed plus for other robberies that were identified during the investigation. Great job to all.

Chapter Ten
The Station Clerk

Police officers are well respected throughout the country. But, every now and then you have an officer that disgraces the uniform. Officer John King was one of those officers. He was a thirteen-year veteran who was well respected by many on the police department.

He was one of the officers that inspired me during my early years on the department. He always gave me good advice and motivated me to do the best that I could. During those days, most of the older officers were good role models to follow. Now some of them had personal problems at home. They always blamed their problems on the department. Some of their complaints I could relate too; long hours, pressure from the supervisors, and other job-related issues. Some of the complaints, however, were just excuses for poor performance.

Sometimes John would complain about his wife. He'd say terrible things about her. She was lazy, didn't want to work, never cleaned the house, and other similar issues. They didn't have any children and John wanted kids. When they were together, you could tell that they weren't happy. I wanted to ask why they were still together, but it wasn't my place. Many other officers were in the same boat, unhappy.

Several years later, I was promoted to lieutenant and John was under my command. I was glad to have him. He was a hard-working officer and dedicated to his work. He was assigned to the station and assisted in processing prisoners and facilitated any operational needs. This included processing prisoner's property. I never imagined what troubles were about to occur.

As a police supervisor, you are always on the lookout for police corruption. You can never expect what a person wouldn't do on any certain day. You just know that at any time, anyone could be involved in a criminal matter. I have seen too many people make the wrong decision that then affects their career. So, as a policeman, you learned to suspect every situation, until proven otherwise. That might appear to be cruel, but it is necessary when dealing with people in our profession.

It started on a Friday evening when we were performing an audit on the prisoner's property. The audit revealed that some money was missing from the property room, approximately $500.

Missing money was not unusual, because there was always some minor issue that was always later resolved. But the amount was unusual. After a week of back tracking, we still couldn't locate the funds.

Once this occurs a full audit is conducted to clarify the issue. At the conclusion of this audit the funds were verified as being not accounted for. Now we had a serious question to answer. Do we have someone stealing or are the funds located somewhere else in the storage area? We decided to conduct another audit and will increase the scope.

During the third audit, we discovered over $6,000 was missing from other locations within the storage area. Now we have a serious problem

The Station Clerk

as someone is stealing money. The only people that have access to the property room are police officers.

Now we go into action to reveal who stole the money. During the investigation we made sure that the only people who had access to the results were the three supervisors in the chain of command. This would keep the information from leaking out to others. We had other methods in place to address the issues, but due to the security protocol, I'm unable to reveal them.

During the next several days, we put in place a process to revealed who stole the money. At the conclusion of the investigation, it was revealed that Officer King was stealing and had stolen all the money from the storage area. It was further identified that the officer had been stealing other items from the property room, watches, jewelry, and credit cards.

Once the evidence was compiled, we applied for and was issued an arrest warrant and search warrant for Officer King and his home. Further evidence was recovered and used against the officer during his trial.

I was very upset once I learned that Officer King was the suspect. I always get dumbfounded when some officers are arrested for committing crimes. Some of them establish bad habits, women, gambling, drugs, liquor and other similar issues. In Officer King's case it was gambling. He was in debt for several thousands of dollars and he resorted to stealing to resolve his problems.

He could have asked for help through the police department, they have some programs to help officers. The department is much better now in addressing police officers with some of these problems.

The judge held nothing back, once Officer King was found guilty. The officer served two years in jail and was released on good behavior. I saw the officer at several police funerals and he apologized for his conduct and wished he could go back in time and undue his bad behaver.

Most police officers are good people and work very hard to gain and maintain your trust. This incident doesn't reflect on the many police officers that work very hard to keep you safe. I have seen too many officers get seriously injured or even die performing their duties to protect the community. Let us remember the good order of those officers and not be judged by the bad conduct of one.

Chapter Eleven
THE GOOD LIEUTENANT

My wife and I were having breakfast one morning at our favorite restaurant and to my surprise, Lieutenant Jerry Scott walks into the restaurant. I haven't seen the lieutenant in several years. He was a great manager/supervisor and was all old school. I learned a great deal from him as how to manage police operations; at the time I was only twenty-one.

He retired in 1976 as a lieutenant. He was on the force for over 25 years. I remember the stories that he told me about his experiences in the Korea War. I really respected the lieutenant. When he would speak about the war, he always looked very serious. The stories made you feel like you were there. He always told me that he lost many good men and friends over there and he hoped that he would not need to send any of his children to fight in any wars. But if needed, he would be proud to be their father as they served their country.

The lieutenant was walking with a bad limp and utilizing a walking assistant. His son was holding on to his arm. He had to be in his nineties, but looking at him, I remembered the young policemen who I respected and the man who was respected by many others.

We started talking and I said I was glad to see him again, but he had a difficult time in remembering me. The more that we spoke it appeared that his memory was getting better.

He suddenly said, "Lt Kittrell. Now I remember. We used to work together as policemen."

I was glad that he remembered me.

As we furthered our conversation he asks if I remembered the case involving the murder of a prostitute that we worked on. It was a case that I haven't spoken about in many years. At the time of the incident, I was only twenty-one. It was a case that I shouldn't have forgotten. It was one of my earlier investigations involving a homicide.

The year was 1975, August, and my partner and I were responding to a police call where a female was unconscious. On our arrival we observed a young woman, laying in the alley. It appeared that her throat had been cut. There were several people just standing around the body and no one was talking. Unfortunately, the area was taken over by the criminal element and this type of situation had become the norm. It was a shame, because many good people still lived in the area. The body was found by two little boys playing in the alley.

We examined the body to verify that she was dead. Prior to the examination, we notify the dispatcher and requested assistance. The other units arrived and the investigation began.

Lieutenant Scott was one of the first units to the scene and he immediately takes charge and starts giving directions to the other officers. I always like working with the lieutenant, he was a professional and always got the job done. You could tell that he had been exposed to many different cases and this was like clockwork to him.

During the investigation, we learned that the victim was identified as Jane and she was one of the local prostitutes. A witness observed Jane earlier arguing with a man in the alley. After which, Jane hadn't been seen. Furthermore, it was reported that she always worked certain hours of the day at the same location. She never caused any problems and had regular customers. She even had assisted the police with other criminal investigations. This wasn't unusual. Prostitutes were some of the best witnesses and assisted law enforcement agencies with their investigations helping close many cases.

Due to good investigation work, the identity of a suspect was obtained. Lieutenant Scott assisted in getting the information. Someone in the area gave the lieutenant a signal indicating that they had information. The lieutenant grabbed me and we go to meet with the witness. She tells us that Jane was arguing with a man and that she knows where he resides. She further reported that he was known to beat-up women that worked in the area.

With this information, and other evidence that was gathered in a short time by the investigators, we were able to get a search and arrest warrant for the suspect. Keep in mind that we accomplished this within a few hours after we found the body in the alley.

We execute the warrants, the suspect lived only a few blocks from the murder, without incident. The suspect was married and had two children. Once the suspect was confronted with the evidences, he admitted to the murder. He said that they were arguing because he wanted Jane to leave the area and go away with him. He was going to leave his family. Jane refused and he killed her.

I learned a lot that day from the lieutenant and the investigators. Methods that I utilized throughout my forty-five years as a policeman. They were great policemen and later great fiends. I really enjoyed those days, experiences, and working with people that I admired because of their devotion to the job.

Some people might say that a prostitute wasn't worth the time or effort that these men devoted to the case. But, as a professional, someone was murdered, and their job was to find the person that committed this heinous crime. No matter who the victim was, our job was to protect and serve the people.

As Lieutenant Scott was about to leave the restaurant, he looks at me and said that incident always disturbed him. She was so young and beautiful, could have had anything in the world, but she chose that profession. The lieutenant walks out the door and waved, saying let's stay in touch.

During the entire course of our conversation, I kept thinking about the young man that I once called lieutenant. He was a great role model to follow. May his remaining years be as peaceful.

Chapter Twelve
THE FOOT CHASE

It was late and we were working jump-out chase. This was the name that we called the operation when we would observe drug transactions and once evidence was establish, we would jump out of our vehicles and chase the suspects. This operation was very successful and many arrests were made and drugs, weapons, and other illegal items were recovered.

On this day we were working in an area that had been completely taken over by drug gangs. The area was engulfed in drug trafficking, shootings, and other vices that destroyed the area. Each day we made many arrests and recovered weapons and drugs, but new people would take their places the next day.

In order to facilitate the operation, we would have an officer hidden in the area. That person would observe the drug operation and, after evidence was obtained to move on the suspects, direct the units to make arrests.

The goal was to observe a person sell drugs to another person. Then identify the other suspects involved, especially the suspect that had the weapon. That suspect's job was to protect the other suspects involved in the conspiracy. The other suspects would transport the drugs to the are to be sold or handle the money. In all, each transaction would involve five or more persons. Our adjective was to gain evidence on all the suspects and then rush in and arrest them

The plan sounds easy, but every case was a great effort on the part of the officers involved. The suspects knew they were being watch so they had to be very cunning when conducting drug transactions. Most of the suspects were very smart people that just utilized their talents to conduct crimes.

When we arrested the suspects, I was always surprise by their education as most of them had finished school. They just wanted to sell drugs and make fast money. The only problem was that most of them would end up arrested by the police or shot or killed by rival drug gangs. There were many others we arrested who failed to finish school and they would always get caught or killed by other drug dealers.

Once the officer was in place to observe drug transactions, we all take our places. The area that we have targeted is completely blocked. If the suspects attempted to escape, we will be able to catch them and make the arrests. On many occasions, the drug traffickers would hire children to ride their bikes in the surrounding area to locate unmarked police units and report back to the drug dealers. These young people were easy to identify and we had an process in place to address those issues. I am unable to identify the maneuver as the police still utilized the method.

It wasn't long before a drug transaction was observed. The officer in the (Operation Position, the OP) identified all the parties involved and directed the police units to move in. In most cases, we arrest the suspects, except the suspect with the gun, within two blocks of the drug transaction.

The Foot Chase

The order was given to move in and make the arrests. As always, the drug suspects started running everywhere in different directions, but we had all the escape routes covered. Within seconds, we had all the suspects arrested, except the one with the firearm.

Then suddenly, we heard the officers that were chasing the suspect with the firearm request back up They said we had a runner, that is a suspect that is running very fast on foot. All the officers that were not occupied with arrests joined in on the chase.

By this time, the two officers that were pursuing the suspect lost sight of each other. It appeared that one of the officers attempted to cut off the suspect by running a different route. This wasn't the proper maneuver. Police training dictates that when you are confronted with a suspect with a firearm, you should always have another officer present, when possible.

As the pursuit continued, the officer that kept his eyes on the suspect finally catches him and the struggle begins. Normally, the suspects surrender without a fight, but not this person. The officer could hear the sirens and the other officers on foot running towards him, but at the time they appeared very far away.

During the struggle, the suspect pulls out the firearm and is attempting to shoot the officer. The officer is unable to pull his weapon, because he can't release the suspects hands, as the suspect is pointing the weapon at him. Suddenly, the suspect shoots the officer, but it is a very minor wound. The bullet grazed the officer's arm.

It was at that time the other officers arrived and were able to subdue the suspect without any further injuries. The officer that was injured, was transported to the hospital, treated, and release.

It was later learned that the suspect with the firearm was on probation and, if arrested, he would be required to complete all his back-up time, which was ten years.

All the officers involved learned a lesson to always be careful and never leave your partner. Two officers are always better than one. I always say your goal is to go home to your family and retire and enjoy life with them

Chapter Thirteen
THE HUSBAND AND THE WIFE

Rita and Tony had been married for fifteen years and never had a year that wasn't in turmoil. People later said they couldn't understand why they stayed together. The police had been at their home so many times that you could set your watch by the events that took place there.

They had known each other most of their life. They were raised in the same area and attended the same schools. Their families were even friends and attended the same church. With such a long and close relationship, you would think that they had it made, but looks are deceiving.

They had no children and neither one of them wanted to have a child. Their lives were no place to raise children. The strange thing about their relationship was that they always attended church and church activities. Looking at them, you would think that they were the perfect couple. No one expected that their life would turn into a nightmare.

One Saturday morning, the couple was having breakfast together and weren't fighting. Friday nights, Tony would go out drinking and always come home and start an argument with his wife and the police would be called. Sometimes the fight would last all day.

On this day everything was quiet. The couple was even planning to go out and have dinner at a nice restaurant; something that they haven't done together in a very long time. They leave the house and return approximately three hours later.

Tony starts watching the television and Rita goes upstairs and takes a shower. As Tony is watching the television, he decides to go over the checking account. He notices a discrepancy in the account. He then goes upstairs to confront his wife about the issue and the argument starts.

Rita stated that she didn't need to explain her spending habits to him. They continue to argue and the argument escalates into a physical fight. Tony knocks Rita to the floor. Rita in turn takes an object lying next to her and strikes Tony in his left leg causing him to fall to the floor.

They now are rolling on the floor as they are hitting each other. Both start bleeding to the face, due to the cuts cause by each other.

The neighbors hear the noise and call the police. It is reported as a woman is yelling for help. Several police units answer the call and responded to the address with all haste.

As the struggle continues, they both fall down the stairs causing further injuries to each other. Rita was first to recover and struck Tony with a chair, causing him to bleed severely to the head. She then starts kicking him to the face and body, causing terrific injuries.

When the police arrive, they hear the commotion and force the front door open. They observed Rita standing over Tony with a knife in her hand, cursing at him, and threating to kill him. The police order Rita to drop the knife, as they are pointing their weapons at her. She complies with their order and starts crying.

Both parties are transported to the hospital, treated for their injuries and released. Neither of them wanted to press charges against the other. Rita went to stay with her parents and Tony went back to their home.

The Husband and the Wife

Two weeks later Rita returned to her home to collect her personal items. She had decided to leave Tony. Her husband attempted to resolve their differences, but Rita's mind was made up. She was going to leave her husband and start a new life that didn't include Tony.

Prior to returning to her home, several family members asked if they could accompany Rita and she declined their help. She felt the present of her family would outrage Tony and make matters worse. She just wanted to get a few items. The rest of the items in the house Tony could keep. The family even suggested calling the police for assistance. Once again, Rita declined any further assistance.

As Rita is about to leave the house, Tony grabbed her and said, "Bitch, you aren't leaving me. I know you got another man."

He then throws her to the floor and starts hitting her with his belt that he had removed from his pants. Rita then pulls out a gun that she had stolen from her father and shoots Tony several times in the chest. He falls to the floor, unconscious.

Rita stands over Tony as she is crying and said, "Mother fucker! I am tired of your shit. I am glad that I shot you." The statements were heard by several witnesses who had called the police once they heard the commotion.

The police arrived, once again forced the door open, and observed Rita standing over Tony, crying, with the gun in her hand. She is ordered to drop the weapon, but she hesitates. The officers repeated the command, as they are pointing their weapons at her. She finally throws the weapon to the floor and the officers arrest her without any further incident.

The ambulance arrived, but it is too late for Tony. He was killed instantly, being shot several times.

Rita is taken to the police station, Homicide Squad, for processing. She never makes a statement to the police. Her parents ask if they can speak with her, but are denied. The father further stated that he had hidden the gun years ago and thought no one knew it's whereabouts. He wishes he would have escorted his daughter to the house. This will stay with him the remainder of his life.

At the trial several people spoke on Rita's behalf, even members of Tony's family. Rita was found guilty of Manslaughter and served several years in jail. Once being released, she remarried to a correctional officer and moved back into the house where she and Tony once live. Her parents owned the home and never sold the property.

Chapter Fourteen
THE TRAIN STATION FIGHT

I was attending a retirement party for Sergeant Joe Smith. He was a good friend and well respected by all. After dinner and the VIP speeches, he and I had a drink together. As we are saying our goodbyes, he asks if I remembered one of our first assignments, the great Train Station Fight.

I started laughing because I had forgotten that incident. Sometimes as policemen, we have a habit of forgetting some of our fewer famous moments.

The sergeant said, "I know you haven't forgot that ass beating we took by that soldier, have you? He beat the shit out of all of us, one man." Then it all came back to me like a bad dream all over again.

The year was 1975 and Joe and I were working the day shift and we were walking the beat around the train station. It was always a busy place to work. It kept you on your toes. There were always fights of all types because you had homeless people, husband and wives, and similar situations; nothing that you couldn't handle, just insignificant incidents.

But on this day, we were confronted with a situation that would take all our strengths to combat the problem and much more. In the next several years I would be involved in many fights, but none like this one. I learned that day to never judge the person by his/her size or shape. The statement "It's the size of the fight in the dog" I learned well that day.

Joe and I are walking through the train station as usual making sure everything is ok. Then suddenly, people start running towards the exits. We start running towards the crows to investigate the problem. To our surprise, we observed a middle age man, with no clothes on, throwing items in every direction.

We were young, but we recognized that we probably were dealing with a soldier having war-related crises. This was a common problem during the era. Many soldiers coming home from the war had many issues that caused them to act weird and in majority of the cases they were ill. We also observed military clothing near him and that he was built like a boxer, no fat on him. He looked like Bruce Lee and Muhammad Ali all in one. We would earn our pay on this day.

Joe informs the police dispatcher and requests assistance to combat the man. We later called him Bruce Ali, because when we attempted to subdue him, that was who we thought we were fighting.

Now we had been in this situation before and always wanted to help the soldiers. We could only imagine what they have experienced in war. Many of the police officers on the department were veterans and always explained to the young officers what the soldiers were going through. So, I could relate in some ways of their problems. But when a soldier is throwing you and your partner around like paper and kicking your ass, you sometimes forget.

Now this guy, looks like he can beat-up everyone that he chooses and he is looking at Joe and me.

The Train Station Fight

The suspect yells at us and says, "Mother Fucker. What the hell you are looking at?" and starts running towards us.

Joe yells out, "Get ready Kittrell. This is going to be an ass-kicking."

Now I know Joe thought it was going to be the other guy. But, how wrong we would both later learn it would be us. I forgot to mention that the soldier was only five feet tall, but after this day, he looked like a giant.

Joe attempts to stop the suspect by talking to him, but he was too fast. Before we could do anything, the suspect turned around twice so fast that it appeared in seconds. His feet struck both of us in the chest. Even today, I don't know how a man could move so fast. We saw him coming, but he was so damn fast. It was like a movie. I never laughed at the Chinese movies again. It is true, they can move like lighting. We both couldn't catch our breath; we were gasping for air.

The suspect then hit us both again, in the chest, with his fists, causing us to fall to the ground. By this time, other police officers had arrived, but they couldn't do any better. He started hitting and kicking every police officer in sight. The boy was fast. Joe and I are still on the ground attempting to get back in the fight, but the kicks to our heads kept us out of the fight.

One of the officers finally was able to get the suspect down on the ground. He had grabbed the suspects body part that caused him to fall. Now remember, the suspect wasn't wearing any clothes. Then all the other officers jumped on the suspect and were attempting to subdue him.

Even with all those officers on top of him, he still was a difficult person to handle. After a few more minutes, which was a very long time when confronted with such a difficult task, we finally were able to get handcuffs on the suspect.

We stand him up and he began using his feet again, even while handcuffed. Once again, the fight is back on. I said to myself, what is it going to take to get this situation under control? We have eight police officers present; you would think that would enough to handle one man.

Then suddenly the suspect just stopped and fell to the ground. First, I thought somebody had shot him, but I didn't hear any gun fire or observe any smoke. There are situations where things happen so fast, you just don't hear the shots. It happens, but that is another story.

Joe said, "There is a God watching over us." Someone placed handcuffs on the suspects feet and he doesn't resist. He starts talking in another language. No one recognized the language, not even the veterans.

It is decided to transport the suspect to the hospital for mental observation. There we learned that his name was Melvin and he was still in the army. The military police arrived and informed us that Melvin was a decorated soldier and was once imprisoned during the war for two years. During his confinement he was tortured and hung by his hands for several days. He was even beaten because he resisted the enemy. We further learned that Melvin escaped from his jailers and was able to lead a rescue team back to the location of his imprisonment and the other prisoners of war were rescued. But Melvin was never the same and was in and out of hospitals since gaining his freedom.

After hearing Melvin's story, I even admired him even though he just finished kicking the crap out of us. I could never imagine what he was going through. I considered the man a hero. All the officers just looked at each other. The sergeant and said, "Fuck it. Let's all go home and call it a day."

Throughout my career I heard many stories like Melvin's and most of them were similar in some fashion. I now know why the veteran officers acted the way they did when confronted with soldiers. We should all thank them for their service.

This story has a sad ending, Melvin committed suicide a few months later. Say a prayer for him. I still have the pictures.

Chapter Fifteen
THE CARRY-OUT SHOP INCIDENT

Joe and I are still at the retirement party and we start talking about the carry-out incident. We were involved in many criminal cases together and learned from them all.

As a police officer, you are always confronted with tragic incidents. There is no way of getting around them. If you have a weak heart, it will be difficult to be a police officer in most cities. This is my opinion. You are always confronted with difficult tasks that only professional police officers are confronted with. This is the job you are paid for and expected to fulfill.

This is a very old case, but still has the effects as if it happened yesterday. I can still see all the faces of all the people involved. In police work, you must learn how to look beyond those sad faces and perform your duties as a police officer.

We are working the midnight shift and we get off duty at 7:00 AM. It is approximately 3:30 AM and everything is quiet.

I always said, "When things are to quiet, it is the calm before the storm. It never fails."

Joe said," Kittrell we haven't even received one damn assignment."

I replied, "Don't jinx us. Let's have a pleasant morning for a change."

A few minutes later we received a radio assignment for a shooting at a restaurant. We acknowledge the call and respond.

I said, "There is only one restaurant open and there is a shooting at that place."

On our arrival, we see several people pointing in the direction of the restaurant and screaming that someone has been shot inside. Joe informs the dispatcher and we then rush inside with our guns out. Prior to our entrance, I see three children crying in a vehicle which is directly in front of the restaurant. At the time, the children weren't our concern; we could always come back and check on them.

Once inside, we see an elderly man on the floor, unconscious. It appears that he has been shot in the chest. There is a woman laying on top of him, crying and saying, "Bill. Please don't leave me." Joe informs the dispatcher and requests an ambulance plus further assistance.

I attempted to administer some first aid, but it is difficult because the woman laying on top of the gentleman will not move. I ask her name. She tells me she is Debra and the man, Bill, is her husband.

As I am working on Bill, Joe interviews the store clerk to ascertain what took place. He tells Joe that Bill had entered the store to purchase a pizza for his grandkids. As the order is being prepared, two men entered the store with guns out and demanded money.

Bill immediately stood against the wall with his arms against the wall. That was when one of the suspects observed a Rolex Watch on Bill's arm. The suspect then demanded the watch. Bill told the suspect that the watch was his grandfather's and it was given to him by his father. Please don't take the watch, but he had money in his wallet.

The suspect replied by saying, "Give me everything." The clerk further stated that the suspect appeared to be very nervous as his hand with the gun was shaking. Then suddenly, as Bill was turning around to give the suspect his wallet, the suspect shot Bill in the chest as his family was watching from their vehicle. Both suspects then ran out the front door without taking any money.

The information, with the description of the suspects was then broadcast to all the other police units in the area. By this time, the other units and the ambulance are on the scene and now we are investigating a homicide, Bill was pronounced deceased on the scene by the medics, even thou it is not official until a doctor makes the decision.

During the entire time Bill's wife continues to cry and some policewomen are attending to the grandchildren. Bill's wife further stated that she wished she hadn't stopped to get that damn pizza for the kids. Her husband is now dead and it's all her fault.

After processing the scene, we leave the restaurant and Bill's family, along with the other witnesses, is taken to the Homicide Squad for further processing.

Later investigation and good detective work determined the identity of the suspects. They were located, arrested, and the firearm use in the commission of the crime was recovered. This was after being issued arrest and search warrants for their home. The suspects were brothers, twins only 19 years old.

It was very difficult to attend the trial and see Bill's family reenact the incidents that resulted in his death. But this was our job and it wouldn't be our last trial. We had many more to attend in the next 20 plus years on the force. The two suspects were found guilty and served over 20 years in prison. I can still see their mother crying in court for her sons; not an attractive sight.

Chapter Sixteen
THE TWO BAD POLICE OFFICERS

The majority of the policemen that I have associated with are proud, professional people, putting their lives on the line every day to save and serve their departments and community. I have seen officers get hurt and killed. I have seen police officers rescue children from burning buildings and other dangerous situations. I even saw a police officer take a bullet in order to save a child. Most of the heroic acts by policemen aren't reported or even mentioned in the news, but I have seen them.

I mention this because this story stains the uniform that we all as policemen wear. Of all the bad incidents that I have known involving policemen, this is the worst-case involving law enforcement officers.

It happened many years ago and I knew both officers in question. When I heard of their actions, I couldn't believe the allegations. I have seen many policemen make mistakes and even with malice intentions, but these two officers' conduct go beyond malice. It bordered on insanity.

One of the officers was married to a very attractive woman. They had been married for several years and had no children. As in most marriages, things started off good, but after a year the marriage developed problems. They both started seeing other people and the problem grew into arguments, fights, and abuse.

They attempted to solve their issues by attending marriage counseling, but that was only a bandage on a very serious problem. His wife had no intention of resolving their differences. She had started a new life with another man and wanted a divorce. She just hadn't told her husband her plans. She wanted to keep him a little longer until she was in a better financial situation. This information was discovered later by the police, once they interviewed several friends of the officer's wife.

Now the story gets much darker. One evening, the officer was scheduled to report to duty at 4PM, but he called in and requested leave for the day. He didn't give a reason. The officer in question suspected that his wife had a date with her boyfriend as she was acting suspiciously when he was about to go to work. The officer later said that she was wearing her special jewelry and perfume.

The officer waited three hours. He had planted a bug on his wife's vehicle so he could monitor her whereabouts. On this day, he located his wife at an address that he had assumed was her boyfriend's residence.

He waited another hour and slipped into the home without anyone noticing him. Once inside he overheard some noise coming from the bedroom. He immediately approached the room and looked inside through a small opening. He observed his wife in bed with her boyfriend.

He confronted them both, call his wife several names. and threatened to shoot them both. To his surprise, the boyfriend was another police officer that he knew and had worked with prior. He couldn't believe his eyes. He started crying and just walked out without any further incident.

The husband, I will call Jack, goes home and starts packing his wife's clothes. Surprisingly, his wife returns home and wants to talk and apologize for her actions. Jack wants no part of her and tells her to get out. The wife continued talking and suddenly, Jack turns around and shoots his wife. She falls to the floor and is unconscious.

Jack starts crying and panics. He doesn't know what to do. He just shot his wife and believes that she is dead, but she isn't; she just isn't moving. Jack then calls another off-duty police officer that a few years earlier was Jack's partner. He tells his partner, whom I will call Mark, that he had just killed his wife. Mark tells Jack to don't do anything and he will be over shortly.

Mark goes to the house and examined Jack's wife and finds she is still alive. Jack asks Mark what should he do. Mark then shoots his wife again, this time killing her. Now Mark takes over and tells Jack that we must take the body to a safe place. I always said that policemen don't make good criminals and I have been proven correct too many times over the years. These guys have already committed several mistakes, not just killing Jack's wife, but they have too much evidence to cover-up and the witness, the boyfriend.

I am not going to tell the other facts relating to this case. But once Jack's wife is reported missing by her family and the police department is involved and investigate, the facts are revealed very quickly. Cases of this nature are very easy to resolve. As I said, too much evidence to hide.

When Jack is unable to explain his wife's whereabouts, the facts are finally revealed. He cracks and admits to the crime. He also informs on Mark. In that the crime involved several police agencies and the FBI, the case is resolved in a few days. The joint operation resulted in the arrest of both officers quickly.

I purposely edited this story. Some of the facts relating to the story are too appalling to mention. The acts of these officers are very rare in any police department. Policemen are human and make mistake, but these two officers aren't even close. They committed a serious crime and went beyond any act relating to sensibility. They are criminals and should be addressed accordingly.

During the trial they both pled guilty and served over 30 years in prison for the crimes. The police department was in shock, even damage, to have two police officers kill a person, premeditated and with malice. This was one of those times when the public took a good look at the department.

Surprisingly, there were few that blamed the whole department. The majority saw it for what it was, two men who crossed the line that were brought to justice quickly and penalized for their crimes.

Even then the technology that was utilized by all the police departments was very good and closed many cases. What is available now to the various departments are unbelievable.

I will not reveal the evidence or techniques that were utilized by all agencies involved, but good and hard detective work brought this case to a closure. Great work to all.

In closing, at the time of Jacks' wife murder, it was later learned, after examining her body, she was pregnant. Many policemen attended the funeral. The family was very glad to see them. I observed several officers cry for the family.

Chapter Seventeen
THE GOOD STUDENTS

Anna Banks was only 25 years old, had a fantastic job, and was very attractive. You couldn't ask for a better family who loved her very much. She was the only child. She had a master's degree and loved her church. Anna had one problem; she was an alcoholic.

She had been in and out of several alcoholic rehabilitation programs, but she never completed any of them. Her family was very concerned and support Anna in her attempts to address her problem. Anna just wouldn't follow through. After only a few months, she would always resort back to drinking.

Surprisingly, Anna had never been arrested or involved in any car accidents. This was very rare, because normally alcoholics always had a driving record involving such instances. Anna always indulged in her drinking habits close to her house and was able to drive home without incident.

There were several situations when Anna was so intoxicated, her friends would take her home. This also helps account for her unusually good driving record. Unfortunately, this only enhanced her behavior and allowed Anna to continue her drinking and lifestyle.

There was one time when Anna was driving while intoxicated and the police had stopped her. As the police were about to approach her vehicle, they had an emergency police call and had to leave immediately to the assignment.

Anna just said, "Thank God," and drove away.

This was learned much later when Anna was interviewed by the police concerning another case.

Anna continued her drinking for the next few months, but it never impeded her job or other activities. She always received an excellent rating and never missed any church activities, which she loved dearly. Everything was going her way, but like most cases involving such reckless decisions there is an old saying, "The bill comes due."

One Friday evening, Anna leaves her favorite bar intoxicated as usual. On this day, Anna takes a different route to the home. She is driving very recklessly and fast. As she makes a turn, the vehicle turns over several times into a ditch.

Anna is trapped inside and unable to exit the vehicle. She is bleeding severely and has broken several bones. She is in terrible pain. To make thing worse, gas has started to leak around the vehicle and a small fire started. Anna is unable to call for help.

The wreck is only a block away from Howard University and the crash is just behind the men's dorm. Luckily, several men and women students, sitting on the back deck talking, observed the car crash.

They all immediately ran towards the crash. One of them called the police and fire department. They reached the crash site very quickly and immediately attempt to rescue Anna. The men are trying to pull her from

The Good Students

the vehicle, but she is in so much pain she tells the students that she can't move. The girls toss dirt on the fire and are able to put out the flames, but suddenly another fire stars on the other side of the vehicle.

One of the female students, a medical student, and gave directions to the other student in the proper way of removing Anna. They utilized some boards to facilitate the removal and this prevented Anna injuries from getting worse.

Once the fire department arrived, they put out the fire. The medics treated Anna and commended the students in the manner that they handle the emergency. They further stated that if they had removed Anna in any other fashion, she could have been paralyzed. The police officers were also impressed by the students conduct.

Anna was transported to the hospital and release several months later. She still needed further treatment to address her injuries. The students were cited by the city for their deed. Anna attended the ceremony and cried as she commended the students. Anna further stated that she was an alcoholic, but this incident has changed her life and she pledged to get help for her illness.

I can only commend those students for their bravery and demeanor in the manner that they addressed the emergency. I say a prayer for Anna and wish her the best as she fights her addiction.

DC Police Stories 3

Chapter Eighteen
THE GOOD NURSE

As a police officer you meet all kinds of people. Most of them are hardworking and damn good people. However, I have seen some people that I wouldn't speak to unless there was a reason; they were just that bad. Most of my career was one that reflected on the good nature of many people. I have enjoyed watching them perform their respective duties in the profession they had chosen.

This story is about a nurse, I will call Jane, that loved her job. I have a different perspective of nurses because of Jane's attitude and devotion to her trade. I first met Jane in 1976. We were the same age, 21. She had just graduated from college. She was working her first job as a certified nurse in a hospital and she loved every minute of it.

I first noticed Jane when a person suffering from a stab wound was brought into the hospital emergency room. Jane immediately jumped into action, not only treating the patient but preparing him for the doctors. I was highly impressed in the manner that she was attempting to comfort the patient. I have been a police officer for a few years and I could tell if someone who serves the public cared about the person in question. After performing her job, the doctors took over and treated the young man.

This was the beginning of a long relationship with Jane. I would be involved in many situations that resulted in a person being transported to the hospital for treatment ranging from gun shots, stabbing, vehicle accidents, suicides, child neglect cases, and many homicides. Jane was a real pro and because of our professions, she and I became very good friends.

I noticed that when a child was brought in for treatment, especially car accidents, Jane would always give it a little more. Not to say that she neglected her other patients, it was always that extra check on the child's well-being, the extra personal touch that a person can give.

It was a Saturday night and we were very busy. I called it bloody Saturday. I was in and out the emergency room on several occasions. It appeared that every case resulted in a person/persons being transported to the hospital from the incidents in question.

My last assignment was for a vehicle accident with injuries. On my arrival, I see two cars wrapped around a utility pole and several people laying on the ground. The ambulance crew had already arrived and were treating the occupants of the vehicles. I noticed that one of the victims is a small child, that I will call Tim. I later learned that Tim was only 5 years old and the only child of one of the drivers.

The witness stated that Vehicle One ran a red light, striking Vehicle Two, resulting in both vehicles turning around several times, striking several poles, and finally embedding themselves against one of the poles.

Due to the seriousness of the injuries other fire department equipment were requested to assist with the treatment of the injuries. This wasn't just a regular accident. Everyone involved was in critical condition, especially Tim. Tim was so critical, that he had to be transported by helicopter to the hospital. At the time, this was the worst accident that I have investigated. In the next 20 years, I would have my share of serious accidents and many resulting in deaths.

In such cases there is a special traffic unit that conducts the investigations. Once the traffic units arrived to further the investigation, I responded to the hospital to continue my investigation.

Prior to my arrival, I learned that Tim's parents were transported to another hospital for treatment. As I entered the emergency room, I see Jane and her team preparing to receive Tim. I always said that if I needed treatment, I hope they take me to the hospital where Jane is working and she is on duty. The helicopter is in the process of transporting Tim to the hospital where Jane and her team are awaiting to treat the child.

By the time they arrived, it is reported that Tim has died. Jane is almost in shock. As they bring Tim into the room, Jane continues to treat the child to bring him back to life. Several doctors assisted, but to no avail.

One doctor said, "Stop, we have tried everything."

Jane starts crying and is removed from the area. Before I depart, I want to thank and say goodbye to Jane. I see Jane and before I could say anything Jane said she wanted to apologize for her conduct. I said it was not needed, that I understand, and I have cried before as a policeman.

Jane continued talking and told me that her little brother was killed by an intoxicated driver and when she is confronted with child cases she always thinks of her little brother. She wished she could have saved him.

Jane and I worked together for another few years. She married a policeman and they had three children. They both are retired and have several grandchildren. May my friend continue to enjoy life and her family.

Chapter Nineteen
THE FUNERAL

There are times when inmates are released from prison to attend funerals. Normally it is for their mother or father. In this case it was for the inmate's mother. The inmate's name was John and he was approved to attend the funeral.

Normally security for the event is always very adequate. The Marshal's Office, Correctional Department, and the Police Department work very closely to ensure safety for all. In this event, the security detail for an inmate who was scheduled to be release in one year was adequate. The inmate was a bank robber who was serving a 10-year sentence and was being released early for good behavior.

The Correctional Department performed a background check on John and no security issues were discovered such as being involved in a gang, threats against his life, or similar associations that would make him a security risk.

It was said that John was very excited about his early release and being able to attend his mother's funeral. John had served 7 years for robbing 4 banks. It was also mentioned that John was going to live a normal life. He had taken up computer repair while serving his time in prison and loved the trade. He was given instructions on how the visit was going to take place and what was expected of him while at the funeral.

It is finally the big day and John couldn't be so happy. It was said that he wasn't known for smiling. But on this day, he was grinning throughout the day. As he is driven through his old neighbor, he points out to the guards everything in the area that affected his life. He told the guards that within a few months, he will be a free man and changing his life for the better. He was just sad that his mother wouldn't see his change.

Once they reach the funeral, John can speak with some of his family members. As he is reviewing his mother's remains, he started to cry. The officers that are guarding John are on full alert, but nothing appears to be out of place. Security was aware of all the family members. There were not many guests. The event appeared to be an easy assignment, but things were about to change that would affect many people.

One of the security officers gives John the signal, indicating that he had another 5 minutes and they would be leaving the funeral. There are two officers standing next to John, who is handcuffed, as he is talking to the family members.

Suddenly a man enters the room and he appeared to be out of place. As the security team is talking on the radio and discussing the individual another man enters the room. Suddenly they both produced weapons and started shooting at John.

Now all hell breaks out. People are running everywhere. The security team is attempting to return fire without shooting innocent people, but the suspects are mixing with the guests and using them as shields.

One of the security officers notifies the police dispatcher and requests police assistance immediately. During the shooting, John is shot twice,

The Funeral

causing him to fall to the ground. One innocent bystander is shot in the leg. Amazingly both suspects are shot by the security detail causing serious injuries. The incident is over in only a few seconds.

By the time the other police officers arrived, the security team had subdued the incident. Several ambulances arrive and the injured parties are transported to the hospital for treatment, including John. The security team escorted John.

No one died from the shooting and John was released within a few months. He had several complications as a result of his injuries. Everyone else, including the suspects, were also released.

The suspects were found guilty of several crimes and sentenced to several years in prison. During the investigation it was learned that John was an FBI informant and the Correctional Department was never informed. Some of the cases that John was working on were leaked to several other gang members and they were assigned to kill John.

Because of this incident information sharing among other government agencies have changed to prevent such other episodes as this one.

John was released from prison on time and to my knowledge, he hasn't been re-arrested.

Chapter Twenty
THE STUDENT

Joanne was a young woman who loved life. She was attending college and doing very well. Great family support and many friends. You couldn't ask for any other blessing for a person, but her life was about to change forever.

Joanne lived in the women's dorm on the college campus and she felt protected. The campus was well guarded and many checks were in placed to protect the students. There hadn't been any reports of serious crimes since attending school. The only issue was someone had their bike stolen, but this was about to change.

One evening Joanne was walking back to her dorm. She was just leaving a late seminar. She was exhausted and just wanted to go to bed, so when she finally reached her room she just jumped into bed. Joanna's room is on the first floor and she never had any unsecured feeling about the location.

After being asleep for a few hours, she is awakened by a man wearing a mask. She tells her not to scream. He then places tape over her mouth. Then he does something unusual. He starts talking to her about his life. This goes on for approximately one hour.

After which, he rapes Joanne several times. She is crying and attempting to tell the suspect to stop, but is unable because of the tape around her mouth. He then throws her to the floor and kicks her and jumps out the window, ending her torment.

She lays on the floor for another hour until her roommate, Sally, finally, arrives. Sally unties Joanne and she shares her horrible story. The police and an ambulance are called. They arrive quickly and the investigation begins, but it appears that Joanne is in shock. They transport her to the hospital where she is treated and examined.

During the investigation the identity of the suspect is learned very quickly. A witness observed the suspect driving away from the school after committing the crime. The suspect was observed taking off the mask. The tag number was recorded and turned over to the police.

Arrest and search warrants were obtained and served at the suspect's home. The suspect had stolen some of Joanne's personal items and evidence was recovered from the home. The suspect was identified as a former employee of the school. He knew the layout of the campus very well. He had been watching Joanne for several months and targeted her. The suspect was also charged with several other rapes throughout the city. He admitted to all the crimes that he was charged with.

Joanne finished school but needed much therapy to combat her incident. She was also injured physically as a result of the attack which caused other issues in her life. Joanne joined many groups supporting women who have had similar experience. She even wrote a book outlining her assault and gave lectures to many groups making them aware of the issues that women are confronted with after such a terrible attack.

The Student

This case was very important to me, because I observed a very strong women not only adjust to such a horrible experience, but reaching out to help others in dealing with theirs. These types of cases affect women for many years after and their ordeals are sometime not understood by many.

I would investigate many sexual assaults during my career as a policemen, supervisor, and manager. But this case I always remembered because of the bravery and respect of Joanne

She motivated me by demonstrating how to take a bad experience and turning it into a positive one. She has helped many women and men to survive such attacks and address the demons that normally accompany the experience.

Joanne married a fellow student and they had three children and are still doing well.

Marco and Dorothy Kittrell

Marco Kittrell started his police career on Monday, June 2, 1972 as a Metropolitan Police Cadet in Washington, D.C. assigned to the Community Relations Division. Six months before entering the Police Academy he was transferred to the Traffic Division which gave him a good taste of police life. Upon graduation from the Police Academy, he was assigned to the First District Sub Station located on Capitol Hill. After one year he was transfer to the Seventh District, located in Southeast Washington. He made sergeant in 1980 and was promoted to lieutenant in 1983. He was reassigned back to the Seventh District as Sector Commander and supervised/managed 4 sergeants and 33 police officers. During his 12 years as a lieutenant he was:

- Commander of a Vice/Task Force targeting and investigating illegal drug criminal activities and prostitution offenses.

- Commander of a Detective Investigation Section investigating all criminal activities.

- Commander of an Investigation Unit targeting career criminals, repeat offenders Unit, (Rope).

He retired as the Commander of the Seventh District Detective Unit in 1995. www.dcpolicestories1.net

www.ingramcontent.com/pod-product-compliance
Lightning Source LLC
Chambersburg PA
CBHW051659040426
42446CB00009B/1206